ST. GEORGE'S HALL

LIVERPOOL

British Library Cataloguing in
Publication Data available.

© Liverpool Museum 1988

First published in Great Britain
by National Museums & Galleries
on Merseyside.
ISBN 0 90636 7 32 8.

Second Edition published in Great Britain
by Liverpool City Council 1995

Printed by Eaton Press Limited
Westfield Road, Wallasey, Merseyside

The City of Liverpool

St GEORGE'S HALL

LIVERPOOL

Loraine Knowles BA, AMA, FMA.

with a contribution by

Edward Morris

FOREWORD

The success and prosperity of the nineteenth and early twentieth centuries have endowed Liverpool with a rich legacy of architecturally distinguished buildings. Collectively these have produced a city of a distinct character and quality on a magnificent riverside site which marks it out as something unique and special in an increasingly uniform world.

Liverpool's visual qualities have attracted a growing tourist industry which forms an increasingly important part of the economy. It is vital, therefore, that these important historic buildings are well maintained. However, many have outlived their original purpose and a new use must be found for them. This not only regenerates individual buildings but can also help the regeneration of an entire area as restoration of the Albert Dock has shown.

St. George's Hall, a Grade 1 listed building, is one of the finest neo-classical buildings in the world and stands adjacent to the architecturally important Liverpool Museum, William Brown Library and Walker Art Gallery. Together they form a Victorian townscape and cultural area of great dignity and drawing power.

St. George's Hall fell into disuse after the Law Courts left in 1984 for new premises elsewhere in the city centre. The building languished for a number of years as not only had a new use to be found for it but an enormous amount of money was required to upgrade it to the present day standards of comfort and safety.

In early 1990 a roof renewal programme commenced and a large proportion of the various roofs covering the building have been brought up to the highest standards. In 1991 improvement work started to the central section of the building and included a new heating and ventilation system, fire safety work and services renewal together with new kitchens and the upgrading of the western ante-rooms. This work enabled the Great Hall and associated areas to be opened for public use in mid-1992. The accommodation has been in great demand since that time.

The next stage of rehabilitation for the building is the north zone which includes the beautiful Small Concert Room on the first floor, the North Court and the North Entrance Hall. Services modernisation is required together with improved fire compartmentation and escape. Sensitive redecoration and a new lighting scheme is also necessary. This work will enable the various rooms to be used for musical and cultural events and conferences.

In years to come the south zone of the building needs upgrading and new uses found for it. There is a wonderful opportunity, if finance can be found, to use the basement for some purpose to capitalise on its magnificent lofty brick vaulted spaces. On completion of these works, St. George's Hall will be one of the finest and most comprehensive cultural centres in the country.

In furtherance of these aims the City Council has agreed that the day to day running of the building will remain under its control but the St. George's Hall Trust, set up in 1995, will be responsible for fund raising and implementing the restoration of the building. The establishment of the Trust will enable sources of finance to be tapped that would not be available to the City Council if it took responsibility for this aspect of the building's future itself.

The future of St. George's Hall looks extremely promising, not only as a cultural centre for Liverpool and the surrounding areas, but as a magnet for tourism and as a regenerative agent for this part of the city centre. It is hoped that by the beginning of the twenty-first century one of Liverpool's greatest buildings will once again be fully playing its part in the City's life.

Liverpool City Council, 1995

CONTENTS

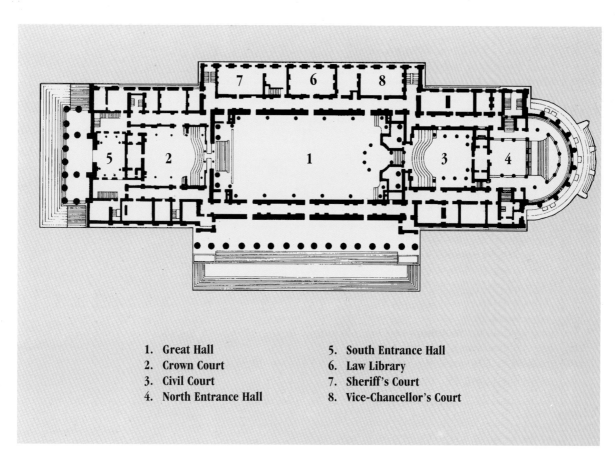

1. Great Hall
2. Crown Court
3. Civil Court
4. North Entrance Hall
5. South Entrance Hall
6. Law Library
7. Sheriff's Court
8. Vice-Chancellor's Court

**ST. GEORGE'S HALL,
LIVERPOOL**

ST. GEORGE'S HALL

As soon as St. George's Hall was opened in 1854 it was hailed as a symbol of Liverpool's greatness and civic pride.

"this magnificent edifice will be a perennial monument of the energy and public spirit, in the nineteenth century, of the people of Liverpool; a place which, of all the cities and towns in the British Empire is surpassed only by the metropolis in magnitude, wealth and importance; and in which, in the quick yet solid growth of its commercial greatness, surpasses even the metropolis itself". 1

The original concept for the Hall, however, was less grandiose than it subsequently became and the period of nearly twenty years that the scheme took to be realised was one of great social change for Liverpool and great social contrasts. *2*

The idea for St. George's Hall came from a group of Liverpool citizens who were concerned at the lack of a concert hall in which to hold the triennial music festivals in aid of local charities. Oratorio was of particular importance in British musical life in the 19th century and St. George's Hall was to some extent designed with the needs of oratorio in mind. In Liverpool, W. W. Currie Esq. was requested to hold a public meeting to consider *"the propriety of erecting a building adapted to the accommodation of future festivals and other purposes". 3* As a result of this a committee was set up, a subscription list was opened and advertisements were placed in the national press. Shares were offered at £25 each, payable by instalments, and by January 1837

£25,350 had been raised. The committee suggested that an appropriate name for the concert hall would be St. George's Hall.

At this stage the committee had no site in mind for the Hall but the Corporation had recently given notice of an Improvement Bill which involved redeveloping the land around the Old Infirmary in Lime Street for erecting public buildings. In 1837 the Corporation agreed to make part of the site available for the building of the Hall and on 28th June 1838, to mark the coronation of Queen Victoria, a foundation stone was laid by the Mayor, William Rathbone, in the Old Infirmary Yard. This stone is thought to lie somewhere in front of the present building on the Lime Street side.

1. Lime Street, 1797, showing the back of the Infirmary and Sailors' Hospital and part of the Lunatic Asylum on the site used for St. George's Hall. Autotype from a drawing by W. G. Herdman. *1*

2. Lime Street, 1797, showing windmills and rope walk on the west side of the site used for St. George's Hall.

Lithograph by W. G. Herdman from a drawing by John Foster.

DESIGN *by* COMPETITION

On March 5th 1839 the committee placed an advertisement in **The Times** inviting designs for the Hall on which it was proposed to spend *"a sum not exceeding £30,000"*. The premium offered was 250 guineas for the best design and 150 guineas for the second best. Competitions for architectural projects normally appealed to unknown architects as a means of gaining major commissions.

In July, of the eighty or more designs submitted, that of Harvey Lonsdale Elmes of London was chosen. The runner-up was George Alexander, also of London.

Shortly after Elmes had accepted the commission and had agreed a plan with the committee –

"there is to be accommodation in the main hall for 3000 persons; and there is also to be a concert room, capable of accommodating 1000 persons, applicable to other *purposes such as lectures and smaller meetings. . . the cost of the building will be £35,000"*

– the Corporation decided to locate their proposed new Assize Courts on another portion of the Old Infirmary ground and invited designs for this building. On this occasion premiums of £300 and £200 were offered for the first and second best entries. Elmes entered this competition, too, and his design was selected out of eighty-six entries. The committee's second choice was Samuel Greig of Exeter. On 8th October 1840 Elmes was appointed Architect to the Corporation for the erection of the Assize Courts thus securing, for a hitherto unknown architect, an extraordinary double first.

Whilst the Corporation had been putting in motion the design for the proposed new law courts, the St. George's Hall committee had been making efforts to improve the number of subscribers to their share scheme to produce the required capital. In view of their difficulties in doing so they suggested to the Council that St. George's Hall should be incorporated into the same building as the law courts. This proposal was considered at a joint meeting of the St. George's Hall committee (which by now included members of the Corporation) and the Law Courts committee of the Borough Council in October 1840. Elmes submitted a design showing the Law Courts and St. George's Hall combined in one building to this meeting. The design was accepted and resulted in the St. George's Hall which is seen today. Initially, it was planned to share the cost between the two parties but later the Law Courts committee decided to undertake *"the whole outlay of the erection and future management".1* The total cost, in the end, was more than £300,000.

3. Elmes' perspective of the competition design for the the first St. George's Hall.
Pencil & sepia washes

4. Elmes' finished competition perspective for the assize courts.
Pen & sepia wash

5. Elmes' revised design incorporating the assize courts and St. George's Hall in one structure.
Pen, pencil & sepia wash.

Harvey Lonsdale Elmes

Harvey Lonsdale Elmes was born in 1814 in Oving, near Chichester, Sussex, to James and Marianne Elmes, in the house once occupied by the painter Smith of Chichester. *1* James Elmes was himself an architect but is best remembered for his architectural writings, most notably his **Memoirs of the Life and Works of Christopher Wren**, published in 1823 and for his **General and Bibliographical Dictionary of the Fine Arts** of 1824. He moved within cultural and élite circles and counted the painter Benjamin Robert Haydon and the poet John Keats among his friends. (Keats' "Ode to a Grecian Urn" and "Ode to a Nightingale" were included in **Annals of the Fine Arts** which Elmes published between 1816 and 1820).

From an early age, therefore, the young Elmes was exposed to art and architecture and guided in taste by his father. At the age of eight he was sent to boarding school in Broxbourne, Herefordshire and from there to a boys' school at Mortlake in Surrey. Elmes' mother and maternal grandfather were opposed to his following in his father's footsteps and taking up architecture as a career but, after a brief exposure to commerce, at his father's insistence, they relented.

As little formal training in architecture existed at this time Elmes, like others, was reliant on printed works such as Stuart and Revett's **The Antiquities of Athens** published between 1762 and 1816 and on acquiring knowledge of geometry and perspective but most of all on practical experience. The distinction between building and architecture was far less marked than it was to become later on in the century and

6. Engraving of Harvey Lonsdale Elmes by T. O. Barlow, 1850

consequently architecture as a profession carried little social prestige.

Elmes, not surprisingly therefore, began his working life with his uncle, Henry John Elmes of College Hill, who was a builder. He then spent some time as an assistant to the distinguished architect Henry Edmund Goodridge of Bath. In 1835 he returned to London and

entered his father's office and was enrolled as a student at the Royal Academy of Arts. He worked with his father on the design of some offices for the City of London solicitor, Charles Pearson, in Park Street (now Queen Anne's Gate). In his **Memoir of the Late Harvey Lonsdale Elmes** James Elmes implies that he was responsible for the exterior designs and his son for the interiors. Charles Townley, collector of Greek statuary, had chambers in Park Street and James Elmes set up a second office here on its completion in 1838.

Apart from the planning and surveying of an estate of *"about eight hundred houses"* for Lord Strathmore in Middlesex and London on which, in 1843, he was described as having been engaged *"for some years"* this was all the experience which Elmes had when he entered the first competition to design St. George's Hall. *2* Whilst the Hall was being built, though, Elmes carried out a number of other commissions mainly in

7. Grange Park, Hampshire

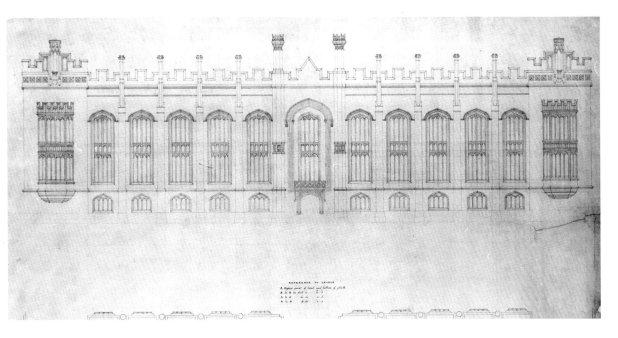

Liverpool and in London. In 1843 he applied for the post of Surveyor of the City of London using testimonials of his work on the Hall in support of his application. *3* Elmes withdrew his application when he discovered that the post was offered only on condition that he give up his private practice.

The most significant public building in Liverpool on which Elmes was engaged other than St. George's Hall was the Liverpool Collegiate Institution in Shaw Street, a school for the sons of *"Liverpool gentlemen"*. *4* Designs for the proposed school were invited, again by competition, by

8. Elmes' design for the façade of Liverpool Collegiate Institution, Shaw Street.

9. Elmes' watercolour sketch elevation of Druids Cross House, Woolton, 1846

means of advertisements in the London and provincial newspapers in 1840. Elmes' Gothic design, under the motto *"tria iuncta in uno"*, was selected out of twenty-nine entries. However, the building committee refused to pay Elmes his premium for the designs or to commission him to carry out the work until they had assurances that the cost of construction would not exceed £15,000. Elmes was unable to give them detailed costings without his drawings which the committee insisted on retaining.

10. Elmes' perspective watercolour sketch of a Church for the Blind, Hope Place.

11. Elmes' perspective watercolour sketch for the West Derby County Lunatic Asylum, 1846.

In the end, Elmes had to resign himself to the fact that the erection of the building would be supervised by a cheaper, local builder. The Liverpool architect, Joseph Boult, later described it as *"a very fair representation of the design of the architect. . . deservedly admired as an adaptation of the Tudor style"*. The interior, however, with which Elmes had nothing to do, he considered *"quite unworthy of the front"*. *5*

The private houses which Elmes designed employed both classical and Gothic styles and are generally considered *"disappointing"*. *6* James Elmes lists these as

> *"Allerton Tower, the seat of Hardman Earle, Esq., Druids Cross for the late Joseph Hornby, Esq., a villa at New Brighton for Daniel Neilson Esq., another at Rock Ferry for William Irlam, Esq., and additions to some neighbouring mansions".*

Hardman Earle was Mayor of Liverpool and a member of the St. George's Hall building committee as were the other clients. Allerton Tower was built in 1847 and demolished in 1933 and only the lodge, laundry, stables building and orangery remain. The lodge has been described as *"a painful mixture of debased early Victorian and classical motifs"*.*7* At Druids Cross only the lodge and stables are extant. *"Redcliffe"* at New Brighton was built between 1845 and 1847 in Tudor-Gothic style while Raby Hall, built for William Irlam at Rock Ferry, was Italianate in style.

Designs of Elmes' other Liverpool work and his work outside Liverpool are held in the Drawings Collection of the British Architectural Library at the Royal Institute of British Architects. *8* These include designs for West Derby County Lunatic Asylum at Rainhill, a Church for the Blind in Hope Street, Pauper Schools in Kirkdale, and some houses and shops in Haymarket and off Lime

Street. His name is also linked with St. Paul's Church, Princes Park, Liverpool although the church as built by A. H. Holme of Liverpool bore no relationship to Elmes' original design. *9*

It is little wonder that Elmes' health suffered – supervising the construction of St. George's Hall at the same time as all these other projects. The seven and a half hour railway journey between London and Liverpool must have been taxing enough for someone with a delicate constitution like Elmes. In May 1847 ill health forced him to retire to the Isle of Wight *"for the purpose of obtaining a little repose"*. *10* In September he departed for Kingston, Jamaica in search of a milder climate for the winter. He felt that over-wintering in Italy would have tempted him to over-exert himself. Just two

12

12. Portrait of Charles Robert Cockerell by Sir William Boxall, R.A., about 1860. *Oil on canvas.*

months after his arrival in Jamaica he was dead, a victim of consumption.

Robert Rawlinson

On Elmes' death St. George's Hall was seven years from completion. Elmes had spared no effort to ensure that the drawings for the finishing details of the Hall were completed as far as possible before he left the country, perhaps anticipating that he was unlikely to return. He had also persuaded the engineer for the building, Robert Rawlinson, who had advised him on the construction of the vault over the great hall, to act as his representative with the committee whilst he was away from England. Rawlinson assented more for Elmes' peace of mind than because

13. Cockerell's Liverpool & London Globe Insurance Co., Dale Street, now the Royal Bank of Scotland

he considered himself a suitable stand-in for the architect. John Weightman, the Corporation Surveyor, had overall responsibility for the building works after Elmes' death. However, Rawlinson's connection with the Hall continued until the completion of the vault in 1849 and Cockerell's appointment in 1851. His close friendship with Elmes is reflected in the correspondence between the two men which Rawlinson published privately in 1871. *11*

Charles Robert Cockerell

In January 1848, a fellow architect and friend of Elmes, William Campbell, wrote to Robert Rawlinson that the only architect whom he considered competent to undertake the finishing of the building was Charles Robert Cockerell. Initially, however, he expressed concern about Cockerell completing it as to him

"and not to Mr. Elmes, would the reputation and credit of the finishing belong."12

Campbell also feared that the design would be altered. Cockerell was indeed appointed to succeed Elmes as architect (initially, on a consultation basis only) and, as Campbell had predicted, he **did** make alterations to some of Elmes' designs. The decorative scheme of the great hall, for example, varies from that shown in Elmes' drawings; the decoration of the small concert room is entirely due to Cockerell and he was responsible for the commissioning of the Minton tile floor and for the siting of the organ in the great hall (Elmes had strong views that his hall should **not** be *"a case"* for the organ).

It should be remembered, however, that Cockerell was a friend of the Elmes family and acted as an informal adviser to Elmes over the project from its inception. *13* In 1843 Cockerell had published his **Idea for the Frontispiece of a Publick Building in England** and Elmes, greatly impressed by the design, recommended it to the Liverpool Corporation for the south pediment of St. George's Hall.

Cockerell, born in 1788, had, unlike Elmes, had the benefit of a seven year Grand Tour which resulted in his becoming a leading archaeologist of his day as well as a renowned expert on ancient architecture.

He is best remembered for the Ashmolean Museum at Oxford, the branch Banks of England at Bristol, Manchester and Liverpool and his unexecuted design for the Royal Exchange. Cockerell's tastes set him apart from many of his contemporaries and resulted in his losing many commissions. He admired Elmes' design for St. George's Hall because he considered it to be neither a slavish copy of Greek or Roman styles, but a skilful treatment of the classical with novel additions. He called it *"...the most magnificent work of modern times."* *14*

14. Cockerell's Bank of England, Castle Street, now the Trustee Savings Bank.

St. George's Hall stands on a natural outcrop of sandstone, slightly removed from the commercial centre of the city, but dominating what Elmes envisaged as the *"forum"* of Liverpool. The choice of this site with its commanding position made an ideal setting from an architectural point of view. Today, unfortunate structures of the 1960s mar its approaches on the south but the visitor who encounters it on leaving Lime Street station cannot fail to be impressed by its majestic grandeur and by the neighbouring group of public buildings in William Brown Street which respect its neo-classical style .

Much has been written on Elmes' inspiration for the style of St. George's Hall. *1* It is a remarkable achievement for so young an architect who had never visited either Greece or Italy. The theory that Elmes was influenced by Karl Friedrich Schinkel's Altes Museum in Berlin has been discounted on the grounds that Elmes' trip to Germany took place in 1842 after he had designed the Hall. In any case he visited Munich but not Berlin. He may have studied K.F.Schinkel's **Sammlung Architektonischer Entwurfe** but this was published in 1841, again, after he submitted his designs for the Hall.

It has been suggested that the source of Elmes' inspiration was much closer to home and may have been the private house which William Wilkins re-modelled between 1804 and 1809 at Grange Park, near Alresford in Hampshire. *2* Cockerell wrote effusively about it when he first visited it and in the early 1820s was himself engaged on extensions to the house. *3* Alresford was not far from Elmes' childhood home at Oving.

1

A closer inspection of the façades of the Hall reveals features that go beyond the purely classical. Each aspect is different in treatment, an approach that only succeeds because of the sheer mass of the structure. The eastern façade (opposite Lime Street station) with its colonnade of sixteen Corinthian columns flanked by two wings of square pilasters with carved panels between, was conceived as the ceremonial entrance. However, the three sets of doors on this side open onto a narrow corridor which leads directly into the great hall. The elevated south portico, with its double row of Corinthian columns surmounted by a pediment, opens onto a small entrance hall adorned with Ionic columns. There is no entrance on the western side overlooking St. John's Garden where the church of that name stood until demolition began in 1899. This elevation has been criticised most on account of its

15. The principal east entrance

16. The north entrance hall.

domestic-style fenestration, a requirement of the law court officials. *4*

It is the north apsidal end of the building which has the most functional entrance and which was intended for everyday purposes. Inside, a flight of steps lead up to Elmes' fine entrance hall adorned with a Doric colonnaded balcony, a frieze based on that of the Parthenon, a statue by William Theed of Henry Booth (1788-1868), one of the chief promoters of the scheme to build the Liverpool and Manchester railway, and fine cast iron lamp stands designed by Cockerell. This gives onto the east and west corridors which flank the great hall. The small concert room is situated on the upper level of the north end.

The
GREAT HALL

Whereas the inspiration for the exterior of the hall may be seen as Greek, that of the interior is Roman. It has been cited that Elmes may have derived his idea for the great hall from the publication, in 1828, of Guillaume Abel Blouet's **Restaurations des Thermes d'Antonin Caracalla** or from Charles Cameron's **Baths of the Romans Explained and Illustrated** of 1772. *1* The guiding hand of Cockerell may also be seen in Elmes' design which reflects Cockerell's own designs for the Cambridge University Library.

The Hall is 169 feet long from north to south, including the recesses at each end and 74 feet wide excluding the balconies, which are constructed over the east and west corridors. The long sides of the hall are each divided into five bays by sets of six columns. The columns are of polished porphyry from Peterhead, Aberdeen with plaster capitals of bronze effect.

> *"...from the entablature on these columns springs the vaulted ceiling, in a single span, column to column, across the hall. The galleries are divided into* **quasi** *boxes by massive piers built behind each column to form the abutment of the vault, which is constructed of hollow bricks, at the suggestion of Mr. Rawlinson, C.E., of London." 2*

The vaulted ceiling

The introduction of the granite columns added grandeur and, in effect, reduced the span of the vault from a proposed 74ft to 65ft but necessitated the introduction of piers from the brick foundations to carry the weight of the roof. The stability of the proposed vault was thus brought into question in 1844 and Elmes wrote to Rawlinson that he was *"very anxious...to introduce hollow tile work." 3* The vault of the tepidarium of the Baths of Caracalla had been *"lightened at the crown by the use of amphorae as* 'aggregate'*"* and Rawlinson's use of a single layer of hollow tiles at

17. The great hall with Minton tile floor and Willis organ.

18. Cockerell's drawing for the siting of the organ across the north end of the Hall. Columns, not caryatids, support the organ balcony as executed. *Pen & wash.*

18

the crown of the vault not only solved the problem of stability but also assisted Dr. Reid's heating and ventilation scheme for the building as it made the whole ceiling porous. *4* The vault was not completed until 1849, after Elmes' death.

The Organ

It was Elmes' intention that there should be an uninterrupted view of the great hall from the platform of each of the judge's benches through to the other. *5* His wish was not fulfilled as when Cockerell assumed responsibility for the completion of the hall he bowed to the pressure of the organ consultant, Dr. Samuel Wesley who had, according to James Elmes

"recommended, nay, almost demanded the entire end of the hall for the monster organ." 6

Wesley was organist of Leeds Parish Church and subsequently of Winchester Cathedral and the leading organist of his day. *7*

The organ was intended as the musical foundation for music festivals, concerts and civic events. After a special visit by the building committee to the Great Exhibition of 1851 to hear the organs there the Corporation awarded the contract to Henry ("Father") Willis of London. Cockerell provided designs for the organ case and gallery which necessitated the removal of two of Elmes' granite columns. They were used as gate posts outside the Hall for some years and subsequently transferred to one of the entrances to Sefton Park, Liverpool. *8*

The instrument built by Willis between 1851 and 1855 broke new ground tonally and technologically and was unquestionably the finest in the country until the building of a larger version in the Royal Albert Hall in 1871. Originally, the bellows for the organ were powered by the steam engine in the basement which fired the heating and ventilation system. In 1931 the organ was enlarged from 100 stops to 120, with a total of 7,737 pipes and converted to electro-pneumatic action. It remains substantially in this form today.

The organ was incomplete at the inauguration of the Hall in 1854 and was used only as part of the orchestra. The public opening took place on 29th May, 1855 at one of the two concerts held in aid of the Elmes Testimonial Fund established to assist Elmes' widow and son. The first organist, Mr. W. T. Best, was appointed in August 1855 at a salary of £300 per year.

Interior Decoration

The interior decoration of the hall is attributable to Cockerell. Rawlinson notes that it was Elmes' intention

"to introduce fresco into the great Hall; or, at all events to prepare the walls and ceiling for fresco." 9

Cockerell's walls are imitation plaster although all the door frames, niches, dados and balcony balustrades are marble. His ceiling is plaster; divided into three sections longitudinally and five across, it matches the division of the bays. Each of the fifteen sections of the ceiling is further divided into a central square with an oblong panel above and below and a set of smaller square panels at each corner with an oblong panel in between. The central squares bear either a coat of arms or a representation of St. George and the Dragon. The horizontal oblong panels contain mermaids holding either lyres or conch shells whereas the vertical oblong panels contain Roman symbols of authority: the

---

19. Detail of the Willis organ, built between 1851 and 1855.

20. Design by Alfred Stevens for the figurative border of the floor.

19

20

caduceus or lictor's rod. The small square panels in the angle each contain a golden square.

The winged angels in the spandrels of the bays beneath the ceiling, which replaced Elmes' plan of panelling around the arches, are said to be inspired by the Angel Choir sculptures of Lincoln Cathedral on which Cockerell had published an article in 1850. *10* They represent Prudence, Fortitude, Science, Art, Justice and Temperance. *11*

The Floor

The encaustic tile floor was manufactured by Minton, Hollins & Co. of Stoke-on-Trent under the supervision of Cockerell. The figurative borders are attributed to Alfred Stevens. *12* The design of the floor consists of three large circles, the largest in the centre. The two smaller circles are each surrounded by four still smaller circles and the design is completed at each end by a semi-circle of a radius equal to that of the great circle in the centre of the floor. It is estimated that the floor contains upwards of 30,000 tiles. *13*

The central circle of the floor contains the royal coat of arms surrounded by rich bands of classical ornament and a figurative border which depicts Neptune with tritons, sea nymphs, boys on dolphins and tridents. In the centre of the two smaller circles are the coats of arms of Liverpool. The four smallest circles contain the Star of St. George, the Rose, the Thistle and Shamrock. The semi-circles at the north and south ends reflect the style of ornament of the large central circle. The rest of the floor is filled in with

"a rich diaper work, divided into panels of various sizes by diagonal bands of plain chocolate-coloured tiles, having an ornamental tile at each intersection. In each of the

21

largest of these divisions are placed alternately the Rose, Thistle and Shamrock."* 14*

The walkway around the sunken floor (which incorporates ventilation grilles) is laid with tiles of similar design. Opposite each of the side doors into the hall is a circle containing a dolphin. Beneath the organ gallery a circular panel contains the crest of the Prince of Wales.

Latin inscriptions with English translations are inserted along the edges of the walkway. These relate to the figures in the spandrels above. At the north end the inscription near the organ relates to music and that at the south end, near the entrance to the Crown Court, to Justice and Government. At each corner of the floor can be seen the motto of the Liverpool Corporation *"Deus haec otia*

21. Detail of bronze doors in the great hall with statue of William Gladstone to right.

fecit." The difference in wear between the tiles in the sunken section of the floor and those on the surrounding walkway is due to the decision taken in the 1860s to cover the central well with a wooden floor to provide a more suitable surface for dancing. *15* This wooden covering has been removed only periodically to enable the hall to be viewed as it was originally intended.

The metalwork

The six pairs of doors which lead into the hall and those which open into the Courts at either end are of steel and brass fixed to marble jambs with a sheet of plate glass between. Each pair of side doors, including the frames, is 12ft 8in high by 6ft 4in wide and weighs 43cwt. The screen at the south end of the hall consists of one pair of folding and two single doors, 21ft wide and 12ft high and weighs 74cwt.

Cockerell's studies for the design of these doors survive and it has been suggested that he adapted already existing designs. *16* In the centre of the ornate foliage design of each door panel can be seen the head of Mercury with a trident behind running the whole length of the panel. At the base of the trident are two intertwined dolphins and near the top a plaque engraved with the monogram S.P.Q.L., an adaptation of *"Senatus Populusque Romanus"* to 'the Senate and the People of Liverpool.'

The pendant lights are suspended from supports modelled on the prows of Greek ships which protrude from the centre of the arched bays. The light fittings are of brass and bronze, in the shape of crowns, with prows of ships, heads of Neptune and Liver birds. They owe their design to Cockerell also.

The stained glass

The semi-circular stained glass panels at either end of the hall have been described as *"gaudy."* *17* That at the north end depicts St. George and the Dragon and that at the south end the Liverpool coat of arms. The manufacturer of this glass, installed in 1884, was Forrest and Son of Liverpool. Although Cockerell was requested in 1854

"to submit Designs for the windows in the hall such designs being as little elaborated as possible"

his designs were never carried out. *18*
Drawing of Cockerell's designs are in the collections of the Victoria & Albert Museum and the Liverpool University Library.

The statues

Twelve statues adorn the interior of the hall. Eight are Members of Parliament: Sir Robert Peel (1788-1850) founder of the modern Conservative party and
20

22. Cockerell's sketch design for a detail of the bronze doors. *Pen & ink*

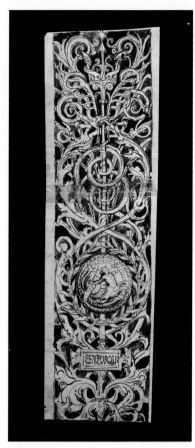

24. Cockerell's rejected designs for the north window of the great hall. *Watercolour*

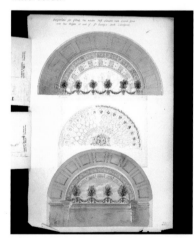

one of the outstanding English statesmen of the 19th century sculpted by Mathew Noble and unveiled at the inauguration of the Hall in 1854; William Roscoe (1753-1831), historian, collector, politician, writer and banker and one of Liverpool's greatest patrons of the arts, sculpted by Francis Chantrey and moved to the hall

from the Royal Institution; Sir William Brown (1784-1864), a Liverpool cotton merchant and benefactor of the Free Public Library and Museum sculpted by Patrick MacDowell; Edward Stanley, 14th Earl of Derby (1799-1869), statesman, orator and scholar, sculpted by William Theed and unveiled in the hall in 1869; William Ewart Gladstone (1809-1898), Liberal statesman and four times Prime Minister sculpted by John Adams-Acton and unveiled in the hall in 1869; Samuel Robert Graves (1818-1873), a merchant and shipowner, sculpted by Giovanni Fontana and unveiled in the hall in 1875; Edward Whitley (1825-1892), a solicitor by profession who held public office in Liverpool before becoming an M.P., erected by public subscription and unveiled in the hall in 1895; Frederick Stanley, 16th Earl of Derby (1841-1908), parliamentarian, sculpted in 1911 by Frederick William Pomeroy.

The remaining four are of notable Liverpool men: Rev. Jonathan Brooks (1775-1855), Senior Rector and Archdeacon of Liverpool and Chairman of the first St. George's Hall committee, sculpted by Benjamin Edward Spence and placed in the hall in 1858-9; George Stephenson (1781-1848), inventor and pioneer of the railways, and chief engineer to the Liverpool and Manchester Railway Company, among others, sculpted by John Gibson and unveiled at the inauguration of the hall in 1854; Rev. Hugh McNeile (1795-1879), curate of St. Jude's and of St. Paul's Princes Park and latterly Dean of Ripon, sculpted by George Gammon Adams and unveiled in the hall in 1871: Joseph Mayer (1803-1886) antiquary and collector and principal founder of the Liverpool Museum with Edward, 13th Earl of Derby, sculpted by Giovanni Fontana and unveiled in the hall in 1869.

23. Cockerell's reconstruction of the Baths of Caracalla, Rome

ASSIZE COURTS

The two main law courts in St. George's Hall, the Crown Court and the Civil Court, are situated at the south and north ends of the great hall respectively. The Crown Court dealt with criminal offences and the Civil or Nisi Prius Court with offences of a more minor nature.

The courts were serviced by a suite of rooms on the west corridor at ground and first floor level and prisoners were detained in separate male and female cells at basement level. Two smaller courts, the Vice-Chancellor of the Duchy of Lancaster's court and the Sheriff's court were also situated in the west corridor either side of the barrister's library. The dual function of the building meant that it was impossible for Elmes to meet the original specification of providing separate routes for the law court functions but as the great hall was rarely used when the courts were in session this did not pose a problem.

Assizes have their roots in the Middle Ages. The term is used to describe periodic court sessions held in England and Wales and presided over by a travelling judge, appointed by the Crown, to hear cases of civil and criminal justice. In 1823 Liverpool Corporation petitioned the Secretary of State for the right to have an Assize Court but it wasn't until 1835 that Liverpool became an Assize town. Prior to this date the inhabitants of Liverpool and Manchester had to attend at Lancaster. For the new judicial purposes the county was divided into two divisions, northern and southern. The hundreds of Salford and West Derby, which included Liverpool, were in the southern division and Kirkdale was designated as the county gaol for the southern division.

Until St. George's Hall was built the assizes were held in the Sessions House in Rumford Street. This was seen as a temporary measure. Judges' lodgings were initially provided at No. 41, St. Anne Street. The first use of the courts in St. George's Hall for the assizes was in the winter of 1851 and from 1868 the judges lodged at Newsham House, Newsham Park. *1*

With the years. the amount of litigation which the courts had to handle outgrew the accommodation available and parts of the building which had not been designed for court use were pressed into service. When, for example, Grand Juries were abolished in 1955 the Grand Jury Room at the south end of the building on the first floor became a court. The south entrance hall was also converted into a court in the 1960s.

The passing of the Criminal Justice Administration Act in 1956 effected the re-organisation of criminal justice in Lancashire. The criminal work of the Liverpool Assize Court was combined with that of the Liverpool Court of Quarter Session, also based in St. George's Hall, and created

> *"A court to act in, and for, the West Derby Division of Lancashire and to be known as 'The Crown Court at Liverpool.'"*

Instead of there being three sessions a year there were now to be eleven, effectively making it an 'Old Bailey' in Liverpool. As a result of the **Royal Commission on Assizes and Quarter Sessions** published in 1969 all law courts above the level of magistrates' courts came under central government control and work started on building new courts to replace the existing inadequate accommodation. In 1984 the St. George's Hall courts closed and the Queen Elizabeth II law courts opened in Derby Square, Liverpool.

---

25. The Crown Court from the public gallery.

26. The Civil Court from the public gallery

27. Elmes' watercolour sketch of the proposed entrance to the Crown Court from the great hall.

The
SMALL CONCERT ROOM

The small concert room is situated at the north end of the building on the first floor. The shape of the room, with half the circle embedded in the main building and the other half projecting externally as an apse, was determined by Elmes perhaps influenced by another part of the Baths of Caracalla — the Calidarium. However, its interior is entirely the work of Charles Cockerell and has been described as

> *"perhaps the most beautiful interior of the Early Victorian period"* and *"undoubtedly the finest interior of Cockerell's career..."* 1, 2

Measuring 72 feet by 77 feet the concert room has a capacity of about 1,100 people. The stage, 30 feet by 12 feet, was designed to accommodate an orchestra of sixty performers and a semi-chorus of seventy. *3* Its acoustics are considerably better than those of the great hall on account of the panelling fixed free of the walls which acts as a sounding board.

The fabric of the elegant decoration in white, honey and cream, with touches of blue and gilt, is deceptive: the 'wickerwork' of the balconies is, in fact, cast iron as are the ventilating grilles along the front of the stage and in the ceiling panels around the central skylight. The pilasters and friezes are of papier mâché. The caryatids look as though they have been carved from stone or wood but are of plaster. It has not been established whether they support the balcony or whether it is simply cantilevered on iron beams. The wall panels are of deal grained and varnished to give the appearance of ornamental woods. *4* Only the Ravenhead glass mirrors of the stage are what they appear to be, at the same time creating illusory reflections.

24

28. The auditorium in the small concert room.

The overall effect is stunning,

> *" a gesture of defiance against the puritanical moralising doctrines of Pugin and Ruskin,"*

Cockerell's contemporaries. *5* It is a matter of regret that none of Cockerell's drawing or plans for the small concert room survive.

29. The stage of the small concert room.

30. Detail of caryatid, small concert room.

HEATING *and* VENTILATION

The heating and ventilation system for St. George's Hall was devised by Dr. David Boswell Reid of Edinburgh. It represents the first attempt at air-conditioning a public building in this country. Reid was also responsible for the heating and ventilation system in the Houses of Parliament. Elmes' original scheme did not allow for Reid's system which was recommended to the committee at a later date.

There was a great deal of concern in the early 19th century about the supposed link between ill-health and inadequate ventilation. Liverpool's first Medical Officer of Health, Dr. W. H. Duncan, was of the opinion that lack of a through draught in court housing contributed to the spread of infectious diseases, such as cholera, with which Liverpool was plagued in

32. Roof space above the small concert room showing the flaps over the ventilation grilles located in the ceiling below.

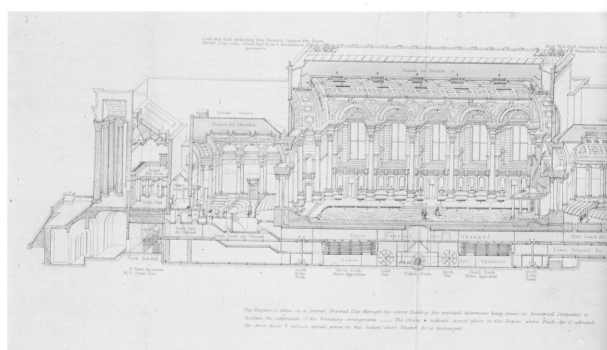

33. Roof space above the great hall showing the hollow brick construction of the vault. Steel has replaced the original timber trusses.

31. Sectional diagram detailing Reid's heating and ventilation system.

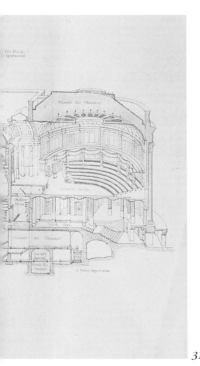

the 1840s. *1* It is not surprising, therefore, that the committee was keen to adopt the City Surveyor's recommendation to employ Dr. Reid even though it involved additional expenditure.

The aim of Reid's system was to warm and ventilate the building for the comfort of users without draughts.*2* Fresh air was principally taken into the building through two shafts at each end of the eastern portico. (No air was taken in from the west side of the building because of the proximity of St. John's churchyard). The used or "vitiated" air was expelled through grilles in the ceiling into the roof spaces above all the major rooms and then through the ducts of the four shafts of each corner of the great hall to the outside. The chimneys to all the fireplaces in the building were also discharged into these shafts which were hidden on the outside by the parapet wall of the attic storey.

31 The air was warmed by five

batteries of hot water pipes supplied by two coke-fired hot water boilers and two steam boilers; the latter were only used in periods of exceptional cold. Four ten-foot wide fans, driven by a ten horse power steam engine and located outside the engine room, supplemented the natural convection of the heated air round the building. The engine was also used to drive the bellows of the organ.

The fans were the only means of circulating air for cooling. This was achieved by introducing cold mains water into the water apparatus and it was suggested that the small fountains in the air shafts would cleanse and cool the air. The warmed or cooled air entered the various rooms through decorative grilles, at the back of the sculpture niches in the great hall, in the risers of the seating tiers in the small concert room for example.

Control of the incoming and out-going air was largely manual and was achieved by a veritable army of workers opening and closing a series of canvas flaps and doors which could be individually adjusted by ropes and pulleys. Access to these was through stairs and gangways in the ceiling vaults and air ducts. Only the judges and court clerks could control their own local environment by means of valves beneath their benches. The system was arranged in zones so that different parts of the building could, if necessary, be heated separately.

An account of the system published in the 1860s likened it to *"an immense pneumatic machine."* *3* Reid certainly understood the principles governing heating and ventilation as his book **Illustrations of the Theory and Practices of Ventilation** shows but he failed to apply them with complete success in this vast building. Nonetheless, despite its shortcomings, the heating system, with some adaptations, was in operation until recently.

SCULPTURAL DECORATION

The major piece of sculptural decoration on the exterior of the hall was the pediment sculpture on the south side. Elmes did allow for sculptural decoration in his design of the east façade — the niches between the square pilasters were intended for sculptures — but no works were executed until after Elmes' death. The sculpture on the plateau and in St. John's Garden will not be considered here.

As mentioned above, the south pediment sculpture is based on Charles Cockerell's sketch of 1843 entitled **Idea for the Frontispiece of a Publick Building in England** which Elmes saw and recommended to the Liverpool Corporation as appropriate for St. George's Hall. Cockerell submitted a more careful and detailed drawing to the Corporation in 1845 which he also exhibited at the Royal Academy in 1846. *1* The sculpting was begun in 1846 by W. G. Nicholl of London (who was also responsible for the four recumbent lions in front of the east entrance) under the supervision of Sir Charles Eastlake, then Keeper of the National Gallery. Around 1848 Cockerell asked Alfred Stevens to make a drawing of the unfinished sculptures in Nicholl's studio. As a result of this Stevens is thought to have recommended some changes to the grouping of the figures which Cockerell adopted. Some people, including John Goodchild, an assistant in Cockerell's office at the time, denied that Stevens had any influence over the sculpture at all. The theme of the sculpture was described in 1846 as follows:

> *"The subject represents Britannia in the centre, and Neptune at her feet; in her left (hand) she holds out the olive branch to Mercury and the four quarters of the globe, of whom the last, Africa, does homage for the liberty she and her children owe to her protection; beyond, are figures representing the vine, and other foreign commercial productions: in her right (hand) she extends her protecting spear over her own productions — agriculture, sciences, domestic happiness, the plough, the loom, and the anvil."*

The sculpture was repaired on a number of occasions in the 19th century and in 1950 was deemed to be in a dangerous and eroded condition and removed. It was subsequently lost.

The bas-reliefs on the east façade of St. George's Hall are the result of a competition held by Liverpool City Council in 1882. *2* The winner of the competition, Thomas Stirling Lee, then aged twenty-nine was as unknown and nearly as young as Elmes had been when he won the competitions to design the Hall itself. Lee had been trained principally in France and he was one of the earliest exponents of the so-called *"New Sculpture"* which combined French naturalism, particulary in the rendering of the nude, with great originality in pose, composition and subject matter. Lee's six panels on the south end of the east façade are the first major public statement of the *"New Sculpture"* and are of exceptional importance in the development of British sculpture.

35. Second panel of bas-relief sculpture by Thomas Stirling Lee at the south end of the east façade. Justice, unwilling to be diverted from the path of duty by Wealth and Fame.

---

34. Lithograph showing the south pediment sculpture as executed. Drawn by Alfred Stevens and printed by Hullmandel and Walton.

The subject is appropriately the Growth of Justice, portrayed by Lee as the life story of a woman: in the first panel, at the extreme south end, Justice appears as a young girl led by the maturer figures of Conscience and Wisdom at the right and followed by Joy behind; in the second panel Justice is now a young woman, nude to represent her purity and thus not willing to be diverted from the path of duty by the two figures of Wealth and Fame; in the third panel Justice, in the centre, is now old enough to uphold the world supported by the figures of Knowledge and Right —

36. Drawing for a lamp bearer by Cockerell, 1854. This design was not executed.
Pen & wash

Knowledge unveils herself and gives Justice the rod of Knowledge; in the fourth panel Justice can at last stand on her own dispensing justice by her sword; in the fifth panel, thanks to this salutary administration of justice, the figure of Justice can hand over her sword to Virtue (or Peace) at the left and her scales to Concord at the right; in the sixth panel Justice finally receives a kiss from Righteousness and a crown from Immortality.

Most of the ingredients in this complicated but carefully worked out allegorical description of the progress of Justice were familiar to Lee — Justice has often been represented as a woman and the scales, sword, globe, and crown were also common symbols dating back to the Renaissance and beyond. However, the ability to weld them together in this imaginative and evocative programme shows the originality and poetry so dear to the adherents of the *"New Sculpture."* Lee's poetic symbolism was not entirely acceptable to contemporary critics and many may have thought it rather optimistic to assume that Justice would ever be able to surrender her sword or scales. Joseph Boult, for instance, wrote:

"Law is an expression of the dominant will not child's play nor amusement for a girl verging on womanhood. . . The artist manifestly does not understand the limits of his art and has attempted to convey in sculpture sentiments which sculpture cannot represent...Ideas purely abstract appear mis-suited for visual representation." 3

Boult's theory of law is chilling enough (though fashionable at the time) and most people would instinctively prefer Lee's approach in which Justice is primarily an expression of morality; artistically Boult's preference for a purely decorative use of sculpture — rather than the intensely meaningful and symbolic role that Lee sought for it — well represented the old debased neo-classicism against which the *"New Sculpture"* made so emphatic a protest. The citizens of Liverpool may also have admired the grand and rather archaic simplicity of the figures, their gestures, their draperies and their poses — with almost all their heads exactly parallel with the building behind; sympathy between architecture and its sculpture was another of the tenets of the *"New Sculpture."*

Unfortunately, however, the French naturalism and realism in the nude figures of the adolescent girl and of the mature young woman depicted in the first two panels caused a storm of moral outrage in Liverpool — and probably without the blurring effect of time and gradual decay even the late 20th century spectator might be surprised by the sharp edge of Lee's observation. A local magistrate was told that Lee's nudes encouraged the sale of pornographic pictures in Liverpool; there was a general demand that the two offending figures should be draped, and even Thomas Armstrong, director of the National Art Training School, found the breasts of the maturer figure insufficiently monumental and virginal.

The City Council cancelled Lee's contract after these two reliefs and only the intervention of P.H. Rathbone, who paid for the remaining four panels, enabled the cycle eventually to be completed in 1894. Rathbone, then effectively in charge of the Walker Art Gallery, was assisted in 1889 by a protest from the National Association for the Advancement of Art which attacked *"the stupid and ignorant abuse"* of the first two reliefs by *"people who have too little idealism to understand their meaning."* None, however, of the remaining four panels contains nude figures and Lee was only awarded the commission for two of the next series of six reliefs on the north end of the east façade. These, intended to represent Liverpool and her Commerce, have no direct connection with St. George's Hall and are much less interesting with the usual allegorical figures identified by a paraphernalia of cattle, wool, corn, ships and nets but entirely without Lee's intense and narrative poetic symbolism. Only two of them are by Lee — the other four are by C.J. Allen and Conrad Dressler, both of whom had local connections.

Since its inauguration by the Mayor and Borough Council on Monday 18th September 1854 the Hall has been in almost constant use for concerts, plays, meetings, bazaars, rallies, prizegivings, fairs and other social functions. It began its life with a three day festival of musical performances to celebrate the opening and on the evening of Friday 22nd September the British Association for the Advancement of Science held the first of many soirées in the Hall. *1*

Minutes of the Council meeting held the week after the Hall was opened declared that

"it be referred to the Law Courts Committee to consider and report to the Council on the best mode of rendering St. George's Hall permanently available for the use and enjoyment of the inhabitants generally with instructions that, in any scheme to be proposed, the recreation and improvement of the working classes should form a prominent and essential part." 2

The Law Courts Committee postponed this discussion several times and turned down many applications for the use of the Hall until the organ was completed in 1855.

A surviving 'applications book' for the period January 1886 to March 1889 gives a good indication of the range of activities which took place, mainly in the great hall and the small concert room, in the Victorian period. Of the 150 bookings the following are a representative sample:

"24th March 1886 Evening concert in aid of District Cotton Porters and Dock Labourers.
1st November 1886. Large Hall. Benevolent Fund Liverpool Operative Plasterers' Association.
5th April 1887 'Special'. Grand Jury Room. To exhibit the new and improved method of applying gas to high class cookery.
22nd December 1888. Large Hall, People's concert. Messiah." 3

The great hall has seen many banquets. On 15th April 1857 a public banquet, for 800 people,

---

37. Liverpool Food & Betterment Society fund-raising bazaar brochure, 1900.

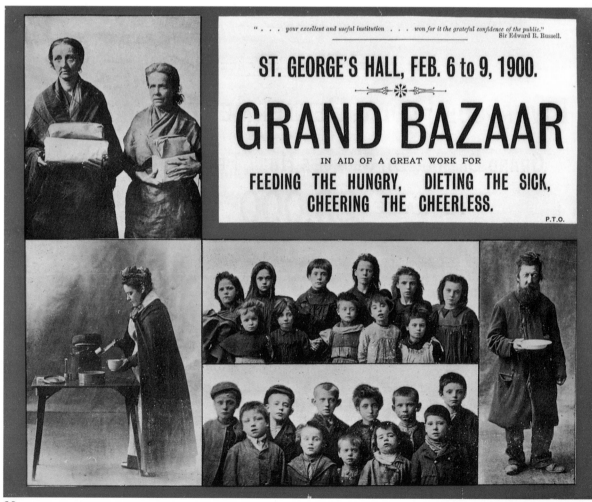

was held in honour of William Brown, M.P., benefactor of the New Free Public Library & Museum. 4 On 10th April 1869 a civic banquet was held in honour of Charles Dickens before his departure for America. 5 Dickens had given readings of his works in the small concert room on several previous occasions. At Christmas 1864 Cope's, the tobacco manufacturers, held an entertainment for their workers in the Hall. 6

The Hall was a popular venue for charitable events. The League of Welldoers held fund-raising bazaars in the Hall in the 1900s and Margaret Beaven, founder of the Liverpool Child Welfare Association, arranged Christmas parties for the children under the care of the Association in the Hall in the 1930s-1940s. 7,8

Exhibitions in the Hall have included a great display of working railway models to celebrate the Liverpool and Manchester Railway centenary in 1930 and numerous others on themes as varied as architecture, education and health. 9

More unusually the Hall accommodated soldiers of the Nottinghamshire, Derbyshire and South Staffordshire Regiment during the police strike of August 1919 and during the Second World War the basement beneath the south portico of the Hall was used as an air-raid shelter. Post-war use of the Hall followed an established pattern but increasing encroachment by the law courts gradually drove out other users. In 1984 the law court functions were tranferred to the new law courts in Derby Square and the upkeep of the Hall once more became the complete responsibility of Liverpool City Council.

38. Merseyside Unity Theatre's production of Arden's "Sergeant Musgrave's Dance," small concert room, 1961

39 Motor car exhibition in the great hall, about 1900

Acknowledgement

This guide is based principally on the published sources listed and would not have been possible, in the short time available, without them. I should like to thank Stephen Bayley for access to his unpublished research on Harvey Lonsdale Elmes and St. George's Hall; my colleagues at N.M.G.M., in particular Richard Foster and Edward Morris for their support and advice, my research assistant Claire Stewart and Val Evans for her design; Nigel Hall for his research on the Assize Courts; the staff of Liverpool City Libraries for responding to my many queries; and the Royal Institute of British Architects Drawings Collections for their assistance; Martin Greenwood for his research on the statues in the great hall.

Photographs are reproduced courtesy of: nos 1, 2, 23, 39, Liverpool City Libraries; nos 3-5, 8-12, 27, 31, British Architectural Library/Royal Institute of British Architects; no 6, Trustees of the British Museum, London; no 7, Royal Commission on Historical Monuments; no 13, Royal Bank of Scotland; nos 15-17, 21, 28-30, 32-33, Martin Charles, London; nos 18, 22, 36, Trustees of the Victoria & Albert Museum, London; no 19, Colin Pitcher, Liverpool; nos 14, 20, 37, 38, National Museums & Galleries on Merseyside; nos 24, 34, Liverpool University Library; nos 25-26, John Mills Photography Ltd., Liverpool; no 35, City of Liverpool Engineer's Department.

Bibliography

Unpublished sources

Stephen Bayley **A Martyr to Architecture — Harvey Lonsdale Elmes and St. George's Hall,** 1977

Published sources

Stephen Bayley "A British Schinkel" in **Architectural Association Quarterly** vol 7 no 2, 1975

Joseph Boult "St. George's Hall" in **Liverpool Mercury** 22nd September, 1854

Douglas R. Carrington **St. George's Hall: The Hall, Organ and Organists** Liverpool, 1981

J. Mordaunt Crook **The Greek Revival** London, 1972

Henry-Russell Hitchcock **Early Victorian Architecture in Britain** London and New Haven, 1954

J. Quentin Hughes "Neo-classical Ideas and Practice" in **Architectural Association Quarterly** vol 5 no 2, 1973

Liverpool Heritage Bureau **Buildings of Liverpool,** Liverpool, 1978

John Olley "St. George's Hall, Liverpool" in

James Elmes **A Memoir of the Late Harvey Lonsdale Elmes,** 1855.

Architects' Journal vol 183 nos 26 & 27, 18 & 25 June, 1986

Nikolaus Pevsner **South Lancashire** Harmondsworth, 1969

Robert Rawlinson **Correspondence relative to St. George's Hall, Liverpool** London, 1871

C.H Reilly "St. George's Hall, Liverpool" in **Country Life** vol LXII no 1592, July 23, 1927

R.I.B.A. **Catalogue of the Drawings Collections of the Royal Institute of British Architects,** 1972

Hugh Stannus **Alfred Stevens and his Work** London, 1891

David Wainwright "Elmes" in **Architectural Review** vol 125 May, 1959

David Watkin **The Life and Work of C.R. Cockerell** London, 1974

REFERENCES

The Idea for the Hall

1. **Illustrated London News**, vol XXV no 703 Sept 23, 1854.

2. Between 1841 and 1851, as a result of the potato famine, the Irish born population of Liverpool rose by nearly 23%; the 1841 census recorded that over a third of the population in Liverpool parish lived in courts or cellars; and in 1844, the first of **Two Reports of Commission on the State of Large Towns and Populous Districts** stated that Liverpool was *"the most unhealthy town in England."*

3. The early history of the Hall is well described by the Liverpool architect, Joseph Boult, in the **Liverpool Mercury**, 22nd September, 1854.

Design by Competition

1. See the Law Courts (and St. George's Hall) Committee Minutes, (CM) 27. 10. 1840 and 30. 1. 1841, Liverpool City Libraries.

The Architects

1. Details of Elmes' education and career are based on Stephen Bayley's unpublished typescript **A Martyr to Architecture – Harvey Lonsdale Elmes and St. George's Hall**, 1977 Liverpool University Library MS. 26. 4 (2).

2. James Elmes **A Memoir of the Late Harvey Lonsdale Elmes**, 1855. Royal Institute of British Architects Drawings Collection, MS.72.036 (42): 92E p. 78. This has been transcribed and annotated by Stephen Bayley op. cit. All page references are to Bayley's transcription.

3. James Elmes pp. 73-81 op. cit.

4. David Wainwright "Elmes" in **Architectural Review** vol 125 no 748 May, 1959.

5. Joseph Boult op. cit.

6. Stephen Bayley op. cit p. 85.

7. Nikolaus Pevsner **South Lancashire** Harmondsworth, 1969 p. 210.

8. The majority of Elmes' drawings are listed in Royal Institute of British Architects **Catalogue of the Drawings Collection of the Royal Institute of British Architects**, 1972.

9. Nikolaus Pevsner op. cit. pp. 237-8.

10. **Correspondence relative to St. George's Hall, Liverpool** (Robert Rawlinson) London, 1871 p. 46.

11. ibid.

12. ibid. pp. 69-77.

13. **Transactions of the R.I.B.A.**, 1863-1864, p. 24.

14. Letter from C. R. Cockerell to Mayor of Liverpool 6 Nov 1854 Liverpool University Library MS.10.5 (41).

Style and Setting

1. See, for example, Henry-Russell Hitchcock **Early Victorian Architecture in Britain**, London and New Haven, 1954; J. Quentin Hughes *"Neo-classical Ideas and Practice"* in **Architectural Association Quarterly** vol 5 no 2, 1973 pp. 36-44; Stephen Bayley op. cit. pp. 49-55.

2. Stephen Bayley *"A British Schinkel"* in **Architectural Association Quarterly** vol 7 no 2, pp. 28-32.

3. David Watkin **The Life and Work of C. R. Cockerell**, London 1974, pp. 69-70.

4. Samuel Huggins *"A Critical Review of St. George's Hall and Assize Courts, Liverpool"* in **The Builder** vol XIII no 624, Jan 20, 1855.

The Great Hall

1. Stephen Bayley op.cit. p. 69.

2. Joseph Boult op. cit.

3. Robert Rawlinson op. cit. p. 37.

4. John Olley *"St. George's Hall, Liverpool."* in **Architects Journal** vol 183 no 26, 25 June 1986 p. 39.

5. Robert Rawlinson op. cit. p. 37.

6. James Elmes op. cit. p. 69.

7. Douglas R. Carrington **St. George's Hall: The Hall, The Organ and Organists** Liverpool, 1981, p. 11.

8. Outside the Hall the columns were objects of ridicule. See report of the Council meeting in **Liverpool Daily Post** 31 Oct, 1855.

9. Robert Rawlinson op. cit. p. 7.

10. David Watkin op. cit. p. 240.

11. **The Builder** vol XIII no 622, 1855. p. 3.

12. Hugh Stannus **Alfred Stevens and his Work** London, 1891. Responsibility for the design of the floor has been much disputed. The Law Courts committee minutes (8. 3. 1852) state *"A superintendent from Mr. Minton attended and produced two designs made under Mr. Cockerell's directions for the floor of the Hall"*.

13. Joseph Boult op. cit.

14. ibid.

15. The Law Courts committee minutes (24. 11. 1859) record the resolution *"That the surveyor do submit a plan of a moveable floor for St. George's Hall to be used on the occasion of Balls etc. . ."* At the front of the 1864-66 minute book is pasted in a printed Scale of Charges which lists the cost of hiring the Hall *"For a Ball or Tea-Party, and including the use of the wooden floor. . . £31.10.0 per day"*.

16. John Olley op. cit. p. 41.

17. C. H. Reilly *"St. George's Hall, Liverpool"* in **Country Life** Vol LXII no 1592, July 23, 1927 p. 130.

18. CM 7. 12. 1854; for the dating of the windows see Loraine Knowles et al *"St. George's, Liverpool"* in **Victorian Society Annual** 1992 p. 37.

The Assize Courts

1. The opening of the Assize Courts and a detailed description of their fitments is included in the **Liverpool Mercury** 9 Dec, 1851.

The Small Concert Room

1. Henry-Russell Hitchcock op. cit. p. 336.

2. David Watkin op. cit. p. 241.

3. **The Builder** vol XIII no 670, Dec 8, 1855 p. 594.

4. ibid.

5. David Watkin op. cit. p. 242.

The Heating and Ventilation System

1. For a good account of Dr. Duncan's work see S. P. W. Chave *"Duncan of Liverpool – and some lessons for today"* in **Community Medicine 6**, 1984 pp. 61.-71.

2. This account of the workings of the system is based on Stephen Bayley and John Olley op. cit.

3. William Mackenzie *"The Mechanical Ventilation and Warming of St. George's Hall"* in **The Civil Engineer and Architect's Journal**, 1864.

Sculptural Decoration

1. This description of the pediment sculpture is based on the catalogue entry relating to Cockerell's *"Design for the Sculpture of the Pediment of St. George's Hall"* in the Walker Art Gallery's **Early English Drawings and Watercolours** Liverpool, 1968.

2. The account of the bas-reliefs is by Edward Morris, Curator of Fine Art, Walker Art Gallery.

3. Susan Beattie **The New Sculpture** New Haven, 1983.

Social Uses

1. **Liverpool Mercury** 22 Sept 1854.

2. CM 4.10.1854.

3. National Museums & Galleries on Merseyside DX/567.

4. A. Hume (ed.) **Documents connected with Public Banquet given to William Brown Esq. in St. George's Hall**, 1857 Liverpool City Libraries Record Office.

5. K. J. Fielding (ed.) **The Speeches of Charles Dickens** Oxford, 1960 pp. 384-393.

6. **Illustrated London News** vol XLIV no 1241 16 Jan, 1864.

7. Merseyside Record Office League of Well-doers ephemera collection, 364 LWD.

8. Ivy A. Ireland **Margaret Beavan of Liverpool** Liverpool, 1938.

9. National Museums & Galleries on Merseyside DX/229/133.